TREATS

just great recipes

GENERAL INFORMATION

The level of difficulty of the recipes in this book
is expressed as a number from 1 (simple) to 3 (difficult).

TREATS
just great recipes
desserts

MᶜRAE BOOKS

SERVES 4–6

PREPARATION 30 min + 3 h to chill

COOKING 1 h

DIFFICULTY level 2

Crème Caramel
with fruit salad

Oil a 6-cup (1.5-liter) pudding mold. • Heat the milk in a large saucepan over low heat. • Add ½ cup (100 g) of sugar and stir until dissolved. Add the vanilla and bring to a boil. Remove from the heat and let cool. • Preheat the oven to 350°F (180°C/gas 4). • Discard the vanilla pod. • Add the eggs to the milk and beat well. • Place the remaining sugar in a small saucepan over medium heat and cook until caramelized, 5–10 minutes. • Pour the caramel into the prepared mold. • Pour the milk mixture into the mold. • Place the mold in a roasting pan and half fill the pan with water. Bake until set, about 1 hour. • Let cool completely. Chill in the refrigerator for at least 3 hours. • Place the strawberries, peaches, bananas, and lemon juice in a bowl. Stir in the brown sugar and rum. • Heat the preserves in a small saucepan over low heat. • Turn the crème caramel out onto a serving dish. Spoon the fruit salad over the top. Drizzle with the preserves and serve.

4 cups (1 liter) milk
¾ cup (150 g) sugar
1 vanilla pod
6 large eggs, lightly beaten
8 oz (250 g) strawberries, sliced
2 canned peaches, drained and cut into small cubes
1 large ripe banana, peeled and slices
Juice of 1 lemon
2 tablespoons brown sugar
2 tablespoons rum
⅓ cup (90 g) blackcurrant preserves (jam)

Peach Mousse
with yogurt

Blend 6 peaches in a food processor until smooth. • Slice the remaining peaches thinly. • Place the egg yolks and sugar in a medium bowl. Beat until pale and creamy. • Add the water mix well. • Place the mixture in a double boiler over barely simmering water, beating constantly, until the mixture is thick and creamy, about 10 minutes. • Remove from the heat and stir in the peach purée and the yogurt. Spoon the mixture into four individual dessert bowls or glasses. Chill for at least 2 hours. • Decorate with the slices of peach. Garnish with mint and serve.

8 canned peaches, drained
4 large egg yolks
$\frac{1}{2}$ cup (100 g) sugar
$\frac{1}{3}$ cup (90 ml) water
$\frac{1}{2}$ cup (125 ml) plain yogurt
Sprigs of mint, to garnish

Crème Brûlée

with coconut and passion fruit

Oil 6 ramekins. • Preheat the oven to 350°F (180°C/gas 4). • Beat the eggs, egg yolks, sugar, and passion fruit in a large bowl until well mixed. • Bring the cream and coconut milk to a boil in a large saucepan over medium-low heat. • Remove from the heat and add to the egg mixture, beating well. • Return the mixture to the saucepan and simmer over very low heat, stirring constantly, until thickened, 5–7 minutes. • Divide the cream among the ramekins. • Arrange the ramekins in a roasting pan. Pour in enough cold water to come halfway up the sides of the ramekins. Bake until the cream has set, about 25 minutes. • Remove from the oven and let cool. Chill in the refrigerator for at least 4 hours. • Preheat the broiler (grill) on a high setting. • Sprinkle the brown sugar over each ramekin. Broil until the sugar has caramelized, about 5 minutes. • Serve at once.

2 large eggs
4 large egg yolks
$1/3$ cup (75 g) sugar
4 oz (125 g) passion fruit flesh
Scant $1\frac{1}{4}$ cups (300 ml) heavy (double) cream
$1\frac{2}{3}$ cups (400 ml) coconut milk
$1/4$ cup (50 g) firmly packed dark brown sugar

Walnut Parfait

Heat $\frac{1}{2}$ cup (100 g) of sugar in a small saucepan over medium heat until caramelized, 5–10 minutes. • Stir in the chopped walnuts. Turn out onto an oiled baking sheet or marble slab. Let cool completely, then chop coarsely. • Beat the eggs, egg yolks and $\frac{1}{4}$ cup (50 g) of the remaining sugar in a large bowl until pale and creamy. • Place in a double boiler over barely simmering water. Add the vanilla and rum. Cook, beating constantly, until thickened, about 5 minutes. • Remove from the heat, add the white chocolate, and stir until melted. • Let cool completely. • Add the chopped walnut mixture and candied orange peel. • Whip the cream in a large bowl until stiff. Gently fold the cream into the walnut mixture. • Oil a large loaf pan and line it with cling film. • Spoon the mixture into the pan. • Cover and freeze for 4 hours. • Heat the remaining sugar in a saucepan over medium heat until caramelized, 5–10 minutes. Remove from the heat. • Dip the walnut halves in the caramel. Let cool completely. • Turn the parfait out onto a serving dish. Slice and garnish with the walnut halves, chocolate curls, and candied orange peel.

1$\frac{1}{4}$ cups (250 g) sugar
1$\frac{1}{2}$ cups (150 g) coarsely chopped walnuts, + 12 extra halves
2 large eggs
3 large egg yolks
1 teaspoon vanilla extract (essence)
1 tablespoon rum
8 oz (250 g) white chocolate, grated
$\frac{1}{4}$ cup (30 g) chopped candied orange peel, + extra, to garnish
2 cups (500 ml) heavy (double) cream
Semisweet (dark) chocolate curls, to garnish

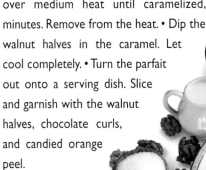

SERVES 6–8

PREPARATION 20 min + 2 h to chill

DIFFICULTY level 1

Mocha Dessert

Slice the sponge cake horizontally to make 3 layers. • Put the egg whites in a medium bowl with 1 ½ tablespoons of sugar and the salt. Place the bowl in a pan filled with hot water. Beat the egg whites until very stiff. Remove from the pan. • Beat the mascarpone in a large bowl with the remaining sugar. Fold in the egg whites. • Brush each layer of sponge cake with coffee. • Put a layer of cake on a serving dish. Spread with mascarpone mixture. Sprinkle with chocolate and cover with another layer of sponge cake. Spread with mascarpone mixture, sprinkle with chocolate, and cover with the remaining sponge cake. Spread with the remaining mascarpone mixture. Sprinkle with the remaining chocolate. • Chill for at least 2 hours before serving.

1 sponge cake, 9 inches (24 cm) in diameter (homemade — see page 14 — or storebought)

2 large egg whites

¼ cup (50 g) sugar

Pinch of salt

8 oz (250 g) mascarpone or cream cheese, at room temperature

⅓ cup (90 ml) strong espresso coffee

5 oz (150 g) dark chocolate, coarsely grated

SERVES 6

PREPARATION 15 min + 4 h to chill

COOKING 10 min

DIFFICULTY level 1

Panna Cotta
with caramel sauce

Oil 6 ramekins. • Place the cream, 1/2 cup (100 g) of sugar, and vanilla pod in a large saucepan. Bring to a boil over low heat. • Remove from the heat and add the gelatin. Stir until completely dissolved. Discard the vanilla pod. • Divide the cream mixture among the prepared ramekins and chill in the refrigerator for at least 4 hours. • Place the remaining sugar and water in a separate saucepan and cook over a low heat until the sugar has caramelized, 5–10 minutes. • Let the ramekins stand in a basin of boiling water for 1 minute before turning the panna cotta out onto serving dishes. • Drizzle with the caramel sauce and serve.

3 cups (750 ml) heavy (double) cream
1 cup (200 g) sugar
1 vanilla pod
1 tablespoon gelatin powder
2 tablespoons water

Panna Cotta

with raspberry sauce

Oil 6 ramekins. • Place the milk, cream, and 1/2 cup (100 g) of sugar in a large saucepan. Bring to a boil over low heat. • Remove from the heat and add the gelatin and almond liqueur. Stir until the gelatin is completely dissolved. • Divide the mixture among the prepared ramekins and chill in the refrigerator for at least 4 hours. • Place the remaining sugar and water in a separate saucepan and simmer over medium-low heat until the sugar has dissolved. • Add the cinnamon, raspberries, and wine and simmer for 5 minutes. • Remove from the heat, discard the cinnamon stick, and strain to remove the raspberry pips. Let cool then chill in the refrigerator • Let the ramekins stand in a basin of boiling water for 1 minute before turning the panna cotta out onto serving dishes. • Spoon the raspberry sauce over the top and serve.

1 1/2 cups (375 ml) milk
1 1/2 cups (375 ml) heavy (double) cream
1 1/2 cups (300 g) sugar
1 tablespoon gelatin powder
2 tablespoons almond liqueur
1 cup (250 ml) water
1 cinnamon stick
8 oz (250 g) fresh raspberries
1/2 cup (125 ml) high-quality dry red wine

Lime Curd

Place the lime juice, lime zest, sugar, and butter in a large saucepan. Bring to a boil over low heat. • Remove from the heat and add the gelatin. Stir until the gelatin is completely dissolved. • Add the egg yolks one at a time, beating continuously. • Return the saucepan to the heat and cook over low heat, stirring constantly, until the mixture thickens, about 5 minutes. • Remove from the heat and let cool completely. • Beat the egg whites with the salt until very stiff. Fold into the cream. • Pour the mixture into individual serving bowls. Chill for in the refrigerator for at least 2 hours. • Decorate with whipped cream and candied lime peel just before serving.

1 cup (250 ml) freshly squeezed lime juice
Finely grated zest of 1 lime
$\frac{1}{2}$ cup (100 g) sugar
$\frac{1}{3}$ cup (90 g) butter
1 tablespoon gelatin powder
3 large eggs, separated
1 cup (250 ml) whipped cream
1 tablespoon candied lime peel, sliced, to garnish

SERVES 4–6

PREPARATION 20 min + 2 h to chill

COOKING 10 min

DIFFICULTY level 2

Mandarin Cream

Beat the egg yolks and sugar in a medium bowl until pale and creamy. • Stir in the mandarin juice and zest. • Transfer the mixture to a double boiler over barely simmering water and simmer, beating constantly, until the mixture is thick and creamy, 7–10 minutes. • Dissolve the gelatin in a cup with 2 tablespoons of boiling water. • Stir the gelatin into the mandarin mixture. Add the mandarin liqueur and mix well. Let cool. • Whip the cream in a large bowl until stiff. Fold two-thirds of the cream into the mandarin mixture. • Spoon into individual serving dishes. Chill for 2 hours. • Decorate with the remaining cream, mandarin segments, cherries, and mint leaves just before serving.

3 large egg yolks
$\frac{1}{4}$ cup (50 g) sugar
$\frac{1}{3}$ cup (90 ml) freshly squeezed mandarin juice
Finely grated zest of 1 mandarin
1 heaping teaspoon gelatin powder
2 tablespoons boiling water
2 tablespoons mandarin liqueur
$1\frac{1}{2}$ cups (375 ml) heavy (double) cream
2 mandarins, peeled and divided into segments
Candied cherries, to garnish
Fresh mint leaves, to garnish

SERVES 4–6

PREPARATION 30 min + 2 h to chill

COOKING 10 min

DIFFICULTY level 2

Sponge Sandwich
with strawberry cream

Preheat the oven to 425°F (220°C/gas 7). • Line a 10 x 15-inch (24 x 38-cm) jelly-roll pan with parchment paper. • Beat the eggs and sugar in a large bowl until pale and creamy. • Gradually fold in the flour and baking powder. • Spoon the batter into the prepared pan. • Bake until golden brown and springy to the touch, 7–10 minutes. Remove from the oven and cool on a rack for 5 minutes. Turn out of the pan, remove the parchment paper, and let cool completely. • Purée 4 ounces (125 g) of strawberries in a blender. Slice the remaining strawberries. • Place the mascarpone and confectioners' sugar in a medium bowl and stir in the purée. • Cut the sponge cake in half and place a layer on a serving dish. Spread with two-thirds of the mascarpone mixture. Cover with almost all the remaining sliced strawberries. Cover with the remaining piece of sponge cake and spread with the remaining mascarpone mixture. • Chill in the refrigerator for 2 hours. • Top with the remaining strawberries and garnish with mint before serving.

Sponge
3 large eggs
½ cup (100 g) sugar
⅔ cup (100 g) all-purpose (plain) flour
2 teaspoons baking powder

Filling
14 oz (400 g) fresh strawberries, cleaned
12 oz (350 g) mascarpone or cream cheese, at room temperature
¼ cup (30 g) confectioners' (icing) sugar
Sprigs of mint, to garnish

Little Puddings

with caramel, cream, and nuts

Oil 4 ramekins. • Preheat the oven to 325°F (170°C/gas 3). • Beat the milk and flour in a large saucepan. Stir in ¼ cup (50 g) of sugar. • Place the saucepan over low heat and simmer until it begins to come away from the edges of the pan, 5–7 minutes. Remove from the heat and let cool. • Place the remaining sugar and the water in a heavy based saucepan over medium heat until the sugar is caramelized, about 10 minutes. • Remove from the heat and stir in the butter. • Stir into the milk mixture. • Add the egg yolks one at a time, beating well after each addition. • Beat the egg whites in a large bowl until stiff. • Gently fold into the caramel mixture. • Spoon the mixture into the ramekins and bake until well risen and lightly browned, about 30 minutes. • Remove from the oven and let cool. Turn out onto serving dishes. • Decorate with whipped cream and walnuts just before serving.

½ cup (125 ml) milk
½ cup (75 g) all-purpose (plain) flour
¾ cup (150 g) sugar
¼ cup (60 ml) water
Generous ⅓ cup (70 g) butter
3 large eggs, separated
½ cup (125 ml) whipped cream, to decorate
Walnuts, to decorate

SERVES 4

PREPARATION 10 min

COOKING 25 min

DIFFICULTY level 1

Zabaglione

with cream and raspberries

Beat the egg yolks and brown sugar in a double boiler until creamy.
• Add ¼ cup (60 ml) of Marsala and beat with a whisk until smooth.
• Place the double boiler over barely simmering water and beat with
the whisk until doubled in volume, about 15 minutes. • Remove from
the heat and let cool. • Beat the mascarpone in a medium bowl with
half the cream. • Add the remaining Marsala and whisk until light and
creamy. • Fold the zabaglione carefully into this mixture. • Divide
almost all the raspberries among four dessert bowls. Top with
zabaglione and the remaining cream. • Decorate with the remaining
raspberries and serve.

3 large egg yolks
¾ cup (150 g) firmly pressed dark
    brown sugar
¾ cup (180 ml) dry Marsala wine
½ cup (125 g) mascarpone or cream
    cheese
½ cup (125 ml) heavy (double) cream
12 oz (350 g) fresh raspberries

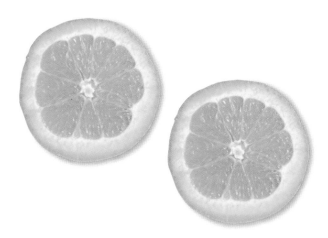

Baked Zabaglione

sponge cake with orange

Preheat the oven to 425°F (220°C/gas 7). • Brush an 8–10 inch (20–25 cm) round ovenproof dish with a tablespoon of the liqueur. • Cut the sponge cake to the same size as the dish and then fit it into the dish. • Mix the orange juice and remaining liqueur in a small bowl. • Drizzle one-third of this mixture over the sponge cake. • Beat the egg yolks and sugar in a large bowl until pale and creamy. • Transfer to a double boiler over barely simmering water. Gradually add the liqueur mixture, beating constantly, until well thickened, 10–15 minutes. • Pour the zabaglione over the sponge cake. Dust with the confectioners' sugar and sprinkle with almonds. • Bake until the top is golden brown, 5–10 minutes. • Remove from the oven. Decorate with orange zest and mint. • Serve hot.

¼ cup (60 ml) orange liqueur
1 sponge cake, 8–10 inches (20–25 cm) in diameter (homemade – see page 14 – or storebought)
Juice of 3 oranges, filtered
4 large egg yolks
½ cup (100 g) sugar
¼ cup (30 g) confectioners' (icing) sugar
¼ cup (25 g) flaked almonds
1 orange, thinly sliced, to decorate
Sprig of mint, to decorate

Pineapple Tarts

Sift the flour into a large bowl and add the butter, sugar, egg yolk, lemon zest, and salt. Mix the ingredients using your fingertips to make a smooth dough. • Wrap in plastic wrap (cling film) and chill in the refrigerator for 1 hour. • Preheat the oven to 400°F (200°C/gas 6). • Grease four (4-inch/10-cm) tartlet pans. • Roll the pastry out on a lightly floured work surface to $1/8$ inch (3 mm) thick. Cut 5-inch (13-cm) disks and line the tartlet pans. Prick the surface with a fork. • Bake until golden brown, about 15 minutes. Let cool. • Spread 2 tablespoons of the pastry cream over the base of each pastry case. Top with a slice of pineapple. • Warm the preserves in a small saucepan over medium heat until liquid, 2 minutes. • Brush the tartlets with a little of the warm preserves and serve.

1 cup (150 g) all-purpose (plain) flour
$1/3$ cup (90 g) butter, softened
$1/3$ cup (70 g) sugar
1 large egg yolk, lightly beaten
Finely grated zest of 1 lemon
Pinch of salt
$1/2$ quantity pastry cream —
 see page 30 (or try with Lime Curd — see page 12)
4 slices fresh or canned pineapple, if using fresh pineapple discard the skin and tough central part
$1/4$ cup (60 g) apricot preserves (jam)

20

SERVES 4–6

PREPARATION 15 min + 1 h to cool

COOKING 1 h

DIFFICULTY level 2

Lemon Meringues
with strawberries and cream

Preheat the oven to 250°F (130°C/gas ½). • Filter the lemon juice through a piece of muslin. • Place the egg whites, salt, and lemon juice in a large bowl. Beat with an electric beater on high speed until stiff. • Add the sugar and lemon zest and beat until very stiff and holds its shape. • Line a large baking sheet with parchment paper. • Place the meringue in a piping bag and pipe drops of the mixture, about the size of walnuts, onto the baking sheet. • Bake until the meringues have dried out, about 1 hour. • Let cool in the oven with the door ajar. • Serve with sliced strawberries and whipped cream.

Juice of ¼ lemon
4 large egg whites
Pinch of salt
1⅔ cups (250 g) confectioners' (icing) sugar
Finely grated zest of 1 lemon

To Serve
12 oz (350 g) fresh strawberries
1 cup (250 ml) heavy (double) cream, whipped

SERVES 4–6

PREPARATION 15 min +4 h to freeze

COOKING 25 min

DIFFICULTY level 1

Pear Terrine
with raspberry sauce

Drizzle the pears with three-quarters of the lemon juice. • Heat the wine and cinnamon in a large saucepan over medium heat. • Add the pears and cook until tender, 10–12 minutes. • Transfer the pears to a cutting board using a slotted spoon. Slice 2 pear halves and set aside. Purée the remaining pears in a blender until smooth. • Return the pear purée to the pan with the cooking juices. Place over medium heat. Add the liqueur and sugar, stirring until the sugar has dissolved. Discard the cinnamon and remove from the heat. • Add the gelatin and mix until dissolved. • Oil an 8 x 10-inch (20 x 24-cm) freezerproof pan and line with plastic wrap (cling film). • Pour half the pear purée into the pan. Sprinkle with half the pistachios. Freeze for 1 hour. • Remove and add the sliced pears. Sprinkle with the remaining pistachios. Spoon the remaining pear purée over the top. Cover and freeze until solid, about 3 hours. • Put the raspberries, honey, and remaining lemon juice in a small saucepan over medium heat. Simmer, mashing with a fork, until the raspberries have broken down, 5 minutes. Strain through a fine mesh strainer. • Slice the terrine and serve with the raspberry sauce.

6 large firm pears, peeled, cored, and cut in half
Juice of 1 lemon
2 cups (500 ml) dry white wine
1 cinnamon stick
2 tablespoons pear liqueur
$1/2$ cup (50 g) sugar
1 tablespoon gelatin powder
$1/4$ cup (25 g) chopped pistachios
8 oz (250 g) raspberries
2 tablespoons honey

SERVES 4–6

PREPARATION 20 min + 1 h to cool

COOKING 1 h

DIFFICULTY level 1

Meringues
with rose cream

Preheat the oven to 250°F (130°C/gas ½). • Line two baking sheets with parchment paper. • Meringues: Place the egg whites in a large bowl with the confectioners' sugar and salt. Beat until stiff. • Gradually beat in the sugar, 1 tablespoon at a time. Fold in the vanilla. • Place the meringue in a piping bag with a plain tip (or use a dessert spoon) to place golf ball-sized blobs on the baking sheets, keeping them well spaced. • Bake until crisp and dry, about 1 hour Turn off the oven and let cool completely with the door ajar. • Filling: beat the cream and confectioners' sugar in a medium bowl until stiff. Fold in the food coloring. • Spread half the meringues with cream and press together in pairs. • Serve at once, garnishing the dish with fresh mint leaves, if liked.

Meringues
4 large egg whites
1 tablespoon confectioners' (icing) sugar
Pinch of salt
1 cup (200 g) sugar
½ teaspoon vanilla extract (essence)

Filling
1 cup (250 ml) heavy (double) cream)
2 tablespoons confectioners' (icing) sugar
½ teaspoon red food coloring
Fresh mint leaves, to garnish (optional)

24

SERVES 4–6

PREPARATION 10 min + 75 min for crêpes

COOKING 30 min

DIFFICULTY level 1

Crêpes
with raspberries and pastry cream

Prepare the crêpes. • Place the raspberries in a bowl with the Cointreau, 1 tablespoon of confectioners' sugar, and the orange zest. Set aside. • Pastry Cream: Bring the milk to a boil in a large saucepan over low heat. • Beat the flour, sugar, and egg yolks in a medium bowl. Stir in the Cointreau. • Add the boiling milk, beating constantly. Return to the saucepan. Cook over low heat, stirring constantly, until thickened, about 5 minutes. • Stir in the hazelnuts and remove from the heat. • Spread each crêpe with some pastry cream and cover with raspberries. Roll up the crêpes and dust with the remaining confectioners' sugar. • Garnish with raspberries and hazelnuts and serve hot.

1 quantity crêpes, see page 28
12 oz (350 g) fresh raspberries
  + extra, to garnish
3 tablespoons Cointreau
$1/4$ cup (30 g) confectioners' (icing)
  sugar
Grated zest of 1 orange

Pastry Cream
$1 1/4$ cups (300 ml) milk
2 tablespoons all-purpose (plain) flour
$1/4$ cup (50 g) sugar
2 large egg yolks
2 tablespoons Cointreau
$1/2$ cup (50 g) finely chopped toasted
  hazelnuts, + extra, to garnish

Flaming Crêpes

Prepare the crêpes. • Place the sugar, butter, and lemon and orange zest in a small frying pan over medium heat. Cook until the sugar begins to caramelize, about 5 minutes. • Add the lemon and orange juice and simmer over low heat for 3 minutes. Stir in the Grand Marnier. Remove the lemon and orange zest and cut in thin strips. • Add one of the crêpes and let it absorb the sauce for a few seconds. Turn it over using a palette knife and then roll it up and push it to one side of the pan. Add another crêpe and repeat the process until all the crêpes are in the pan. • Transfer the crêpes and sauce to a serving dish. Sprinkle with the zest. • Drizzle with the Armagnac, holding a lit match near the alcohol so that it catches light. • Serve at once.

1 quantity crêpes, see page 28
$1/4$ cup (50 g) sugar
1 tablespoon butter
Zest of $1/2$ lemon, removed with a sharp knife
Zest of 1 orange, removed with a sharp knife
2 tablespoons freshly squeezed lemon juice
$1/3$ cup (90 ml) freshly squeezed orange juice
3 tablespoons Grand Marnier
$1/4$ cup (60 ml) Armagnac

SERVES 6–8

PREPARATION 15 min + 1 h to rest

COOKING 30 min

DIFFICULTY level 2

Cherry Crêpes

Crêpes: Sift the flour and salt into a medium bowl. Beat in the eggs, one at a time. Gradually add the milk, beating until smooth. • Set the batter aside for 1 hour to rest. • Melt 1 teaspoon of butter in a crêpe pan and add 2–3 tablespoons of the batter. Swivel the pan so that the batter coats the base evenly. Cook until lightly browned, about 2 minutes. • Turn the crêpe using a palette knife and cook until lightly browned, about 2 minutes. Slip onto a plate. • Repeat this process until all the batter is cooked. • Filling: Place the cherries in a medium saucepan over medium heat. Add the water and sugar. Bring to a boil then lower the heat. Simmer until the sauce has thickened to make a syrup, about 10 minutes. Remove from the heat and let cool. • Stir in the Grand Marnier. • Spread each crêpe with some of the cherry sauce. Fold the filled crêpes in half and then in half again to form triangles. • Dust with confectioners' sugar and serve.

Crêpes
4 large eggs
Pinch of salt
$\frac{1}{2}$ cup (75 g) all-purpose (plain) flour
1 cup (250 ml) milk
3–4 tablespoons butter

Filling
14 oz (400 g) cherries, pitted
1 cup (250 ml) water
$\frac{1}{2}$ cup (100 g) sugar
$\frac{1}{4}$ cup (60 ml) Grand Marnier
2–4 tablespoons confectioners' (icing) sugar, to dust

Apple Crêpes

Prepare the crêpes. • Preheat the oven to 400°F (200°C/gas 6). • Pastry Cream: Bring the milk to a boil in a large saucepan over low heat. • Beat the flour, sugar, and egg yolks in a medium bowl. • Add the boiling milk, beating constantly. Return to the saucepan. Simmer over low heat, stirring constantly, until thickened, 3–5 minutes. Remove from the heat and let cool. • Melt the butter in a saucepan over medium heat. Add the apples, 2 tablespoons of sugar, and 2 tablespoons of rum. Simmer until the apples are tender, about 5 minutes. Stir in the cinnamon and remove from the heat. Let cool slightly. • Stir the apple mixture into the pastry cream. • Spread each crêpe with some of the cream. Roll up the crêpes and place in a greased ovenproof dish. Sprinkle with the remaining sugar and bake until the sugar has caramelized, 10–15 minutes. • Drizzle with the remaining rum, holding a lit match near the alcohol so that it catches light. Serve at once.

1 quantity crêpes, see page 28

Pastry Cream
1 1/4 cups (300 ml) milk
2 tablespoons all-purpose (plain) flour
1/4 cup (50 g) sugar
2 large egg yolks

Filling
2 tablespoons butter
3 apples, peeled, cored, and sliced
1/3 cup (70 g) sugar
1/3 cup (90 ml) rum
1 teaspoon ground cinnamon

SERVES 4–6

PREPARATION 10 min + 75 min for crêpes

COOKING 30 min

DIFFICULTY level 1

Crêpes
with redcurrants and rum

Prepare the crêpes. • Melt the preserves in a small saucepan over low heat. Stir in the rum. Remove from the heat. • Beat the cream in a large bowl until stiff. • Spread each crêpe with a layer of preserves. Fold in half and then in half again to form triangles. • Arrange on serving dishes. • Decorate with whipped cream and the fresh red currants. • Serve at once.

1 quantity crêpes, see page 28

1½ cups (375 g) redcurrant (or other berry fruit) preserves (jam)
1 tablespoon rum
½ cup (125 ml) heavy (double) cream
Fresh redcurrants, to garnish

SERVES 6–8

PREPARATION 30 min + 7 h to chill

COOKING 1 h

DIFFICULTY level 1

Cheesecake
with sour cream

Butter a 10-inch (25-cm) springform pan. • Crust: Melt the butter and mix with the crumbs, sugar, cinnamon, and ginger in a medium bowl. • Press into the bottom and partway up the sides of the prepared pan. Refrigerate for 1 hour. • Filling: Preheat the oven to 375°F (190°C/gas 5). • Beat the cream cheese, sugar, vanilla, and almond extract in a large bowl with an electric mixer at medium speed until smooth. • Add the eggs, one at a time, beating until just blended after each addition. • With mixer at low speed, add the cinnamon, ginger, and nutmeg. • Spoon the filling into the crust. • Bake until set, about 50 minutes. • Cool the cake in the pan for 10 minutes. • Topping: Beat together the sour cream, sugar, and vanilla in a medium bowl. Spread over the cheesecake. • Bake until set, about 10 minutes. • Cool in the pan on a rack. • Refrigerate for 6 hours. Loosen and remove the pan sides to serve.

Crust
4 tablespoons butter
2 cups (300 g) graham cracker (digestive biscuit) crumbs
6 tablespoons raw sugar
1 teaspoon ground cinnamon
1 teaspoon ground ginger

Filling
1½ lb (750 g) cream cheese
1 cup (200 g) sugar
2 teaspoons vanilla extract (essence)
½ teaspoon almond extract
3 large eggs
1 teaspoon ground cinnamon
1 teaspoon ground ginger
½ teaspoon ground nutmeg

Topping
2 cups (500 ml) sour cream
1 tablespoon sugar
1 teaspoon vanilla extract (essence)

Strawberry Pie

Pastry: Sift the flour and salt into a large bowl. Add the sugar and lemon zest. • Rub in the butter using your fingertips until the mixture resembles bread crumbs. • Add the egg and port and mix to make a smooth dough. • Wrap in plastic wrap (cling film) and chill in the refrigerator for 30 minutes. • Preheat the oven to 400°F (200°C/gas 6). • Butter a 10-inch (25-cm) pie plate. • Roll out the pastry on a floured work surface and use it to line the prepared pan. Cover with waxed paper and fill with dried beans or pie weights. • Bake blind for 30 minutes. • Let cool. Discard the beans and waxed paper. • Pastry Cream: Bring the milk to a boil in a large saucepan. • Beat the egg yolks, flour, and sugar in a large bowl until pale and creamy. • Add the hot milk and beat well. Return the mixture to the pan and simmer, stirring constantly, until thickened, 5–7 minutes. • Add the vanilla. • Remove from the heat and let cool slightly. • Pour into the pastry case. Let cool a little then chill in the refrigerator for 1 hour. • Top with the strawberries and brush with the apricot preserves.

Pastry

1 1/3 cups (200 g) all-purpose (plain) flour

1/8 teaspoon salt

1/2 cup (100 g) sugar

Finely grated zest of 1 lemon

1/3 cup (90 g) cold butter, cut up

1 large egg, lightly beaten

2 tablespoons port

Pastry Cream

1 1/4 cups (310 ml) milk

2 large egg yolks

2 tablespoons all-purpose (plain) flour

1/2 cup (100 g) sugar

1 teaspoon vanilla extract (essence)

12 oz (350 g) strawberries, sliced

1/2 cup (125 g) apricot preserves (jam), melted

Pineapple Soufflés

Preheat the oven to 325°F (170°C/gas 3). • Oil 6 ramekins. • Soufflés: Place the pineapple in a saucepan over high heat until all the juice has evaporated, 1–2 minutes. • Place in a food processor and chop until smooth. • Bring the milk, cream, and lemon zest to a boil in a saucepan over medium heat. • Beat 1 egg and 2 egg yolks with the flour and sugar in a saucepan. • Add the boiling milk mixture, stirring constantly. • Cook over low heat, stirring constantly, until thickened, 5–7 minutes. • Remove from the heat and stir in the butter and remaining egg yolk. Let cool. • Add the pineapple purée. • Beat the egg whites in a large bowl until stiff. Fold into the pineapple mixture. • Spoon the mixture into the ramekins. • Bake until well risen and lightly browned, 20 minutes. • Sauce: Chop three-quarters of the pineapple with the sugar in a food processor until smooth. Chop the remaining pineapple into small pieces. • Add the crème de cassis and the reserved pineapple. • Dust the soufflés with confectioners' sugar and serve hot with the pineapple sauce.

Soufflés
8 oz (250 g) canned pineapple, drained
1 cup (250 ml) milk
1/4 cup (60 ml) heavy (double) cream
Finely grated zest of 1/2 lemon
3 large eggs, separated + 4 egg whites
1/2 cup (75 g) all-purpose (plain) flour
1/2 cup (100 g) sugar
2 tablespoons butter

Sauce
8 oz (250 g) canned pineapple, drained
1/4 cup (50 g) sugar
1 tablespoon crème de cassis

2 tablespoons confectioners' (icing) sugar

SERVES 4–6

PREPARATION 20 min

COOKING 1 h

DIFFICULTY level 2

Rice Soufflés

Preheat the oven to 325°F (170°C/gas 3). • Oil 4–6 ramekins and sprinkle each one with a little sugar. • Bring the milk to a boil with the lemon zest in a large saucepan over medium heat. • Add the rice and simmer until tender and the milk is absorbed, about 25 minutes. • Remove from the heat and let cool slightly. Remove and discard the lemon zest. • Add the egg yolks one at a time, beating well after each addition. • Stir in the butter, rum, and sugar. Let cool completely. • Beat the egg whites in a large bowl until stiff. • Fold into the rice mixture. • Spoon the mixture into the prepared ramekins. • Bake until well risen and lightly browned, 20–25 minutes. • Dust with confectioners' sugar and serve hot.

4 cups (1 liter) milk

Zest of 1 lemon, removed with a sharp knife

1 cup (200 g) pudding rice

5 large eggs, separated

1/3 cup (90 g) butter

1 tablespoon rum

3/4 cup (150 g) sugar

2 tablespoons confectioners' (icing) sugar

SERVES 6–8

PREPARATION 25 min

COOKING 30 min

DIFFICULTY level 1

Blackberry Tart

Preheat the oven to 350°F (180°C/gas 4). • Grease a 10-inch (25-cm) tart pan. • Sift both flours, baking powder, and salt into a large bowl. • Beat butter and sugar in a large bowl until pale and creamy. • Add the egg and 2 egg yolks and beat until just combined. • Gradually beat in the mixed dry ingredients. • Roll out two-thirds of the pastry on a lightly floured work surface into a 12-inch (30-cm) disk. Line the pan, trimming away any excess from around the edges. Prick with a fork. • Spread with the preserves. • Roll out the remaining pastry to ¼ inch (5 mm) thick. Cut it into strips and decorate the tart in a lattice pattern. • Brush with the remaining lightly beaten egg yolk. • Bake until the pastry is golden brown, about 30 minutes. • Serve hot or at room temperature.

1⅓ cups (200 g) whole-wheat (wholemeal) flour
⅔ cup (100 g) all-purpose (plain) flour
1 teaspoon baking powder
⅛ teaspoon salt
1 cup (250 g) butter, softened
1 cup (200 g) firmly packed brown sugar
1 large egg
3 large egg yolks
1 cup (300 g) blackberry preserves (jam)

Berry Fruit Tart

Preheat the oven to 375°F (190°C/gas 5). • Grease a 10-inch (25-cm) tart pan. • Roll out the pastry on a lightly floured work surface to ¼ inch (5 mm) thick. • Line the pan with the pastry. Trim off and discard any excess. Prick with a fork. • Bake blind until golden brown, 15–20 minutes. • Remove from the oven and let cool. • Bring the milk and lemon zest to a boil over medium heat. • Beat the egg yolks, sugar, and flour in a large bowl until smooth. • Gradually beat in the milk. • Return to the saucepan over low heat, stirring constantly, until thickened, 5–7 minutes. • Remove from the heat and stir in the Kirsch. Let cool. • Transfer the pastry case to a serving dish and spread with the pastry cream. Arrange the raspberries and blackberries on top. Warm the preserves in a small saucepan over medium heat and brush over the fruit.

14 oz (400 g) frozen sweet short crust pastry, thawed

3 cups (750 ml) milk

Finely grated zest of 1 lemon

2 large egg yolks

¼ cup (50 g) sugar

¼ cup (30 g) all-purpose (plain) flour

1 tablespoon kirsch (cherry liqueur)

5 oz (150 g) fresh raspberries

5 oz (150 g) fresh blackberries

¼ cup (60 g) apricot preserves (jam)

SERVES 6–8

PREPARATION 40 min + 30 min to chill

COOKING 30 min

DIFFICULTY level 2

Creamy Pie
with fresh fruit topping

Sift the flour, sugar, and salt into a large bowl. Mix the butter in with your fingertips until the mixture resembles coarse crumbs. • Add the egg yolk and water and mix to form a smooth dough. Shape into a ball, wrap in plastic wrap (cling film), and refrigerate for 30 minutes. • Preheat the oven to 375°F (190°C/gas 5). • Butter a 9-inch (23-cm) tart pan. Roll the dough out on a lightly floured work surface to a 12-inch (30-cm) disk. • Line with the pastry, trimming the edges. • Line the pastry shell with a sheet of waxed paper and fill with dried beans or pie weights. • Bake for 15 minutes. Discard the paper and beans or pie weights. Bake until crisp and golden brown, about 15 minutes. • Let cool completely. • Topping: Spoon the pastry cream into the pastry case. Arrange the fruit on top and brush with the warm preserves.

Pastry
1 cup (150 g) all-purpose (plain) flour
2 tablespoons sugar
1/8 teaspoon salt
1/3 cup (90 g) cold butter, cut up
1 large egg yolk
1 tablespoon ice water

Topping
1 quantity pastry cream
  (see page 34)
2 cups (500 g) mixed sliced fresh fruit
  or whole berries
1/3 cup (90 g) apricot preserves (jam),
  warmed

Kiwi Tart

Preheat the oven to 350°F (180°C/gas 4). • Grease a 10-inch (25 - cm) pie pan. • Roll out the pastry on a lightly floured work surface to $1/4$ inch (5 mm) thick. Line the pan with the pastry. Trim off and discard any excess. Prick with a fork. • Bake until pale gold, about 15 minutes. • Arrange the sliced kiwi in the pastry case. Beat the cream, eggs, brandy, and half the sugar in a bowl until smooth. Pour the mixture over the kiwi. • Bake until the cream and egg mixture is set, about 20 minutes. • Preheat the broiler (grill) on a high setting. • Sprinkle the tart with the remaining sugar. • Place under the broiler until the sugar begins to caramelize, 3–4 minutes. • Serve warm.

14 oz (400 g) frozen sweet short crust pastry, thawed

10 large kiwi fruit, peeled and sliced

Generous $1/3$ cup (100 ml) heavy (double) cream

2 large eggs, lightly beaten

2 tablespoons brandy

1 cup (200 g) sugar

Mixed Fruit Tart

Preheat the oven to 350°F (180°C/gas 4). • Grease a 10-inch (25-cm) pie pan. • Roll out the pastry on a lightly floured work surface to 1/4 inch (5 mm) thick. Line the pan with the pastry. Trim off and discard any excess. • Spread the pastry cream over the pastry case. Arrange the fruit over the pastry cream. • Bake until the pastry is golden brown and the fruit is tender, 40–50 minutes. • Warm the preserves in a small saucepan over medium heat. Brush the tart with the warm preserves.• Serve hot.

14 oz (400 g) frozen sweet short crust pastry, thawed

1 quantity pastry cream (see page 34)

8 oz (250 g) canned peaches, drained and sliced

2 apples, peeled, cored, and sliced

2 pears, peeled, cored, and sliced

1/4 cup (60 g) apricot preserves (jam)

SERVES 6–8

PREPARATION 15 min

COOKING 25 min

DIFFICULTY level 1

Baklava

with almonds and walnuts

Preheat the oven to 400°F (200°C/gas 6). • Butter a jelly-roll pan. • Lay the sheets of dough out flat and cover with waxed paper and a damp kitchen towel. (This will stop them from drying out.) • Mix the almonds, walnuts, cinnamon, and cloves in a large bowl. • Fit one phyllo sheet in the pan and brush with butter. Fit another sheet on top and brush with butter. Place another 3 sheets on top and sprinkle with the nut mixture. Brush each sheet with more butter. Repeat until all the almond mixture is used up, finishing with a layer of pastry. • Cut the baklava into squares and drizzle with the remaining butter. • Bake until golden brown, about 30 minutes. • Syrup: Place all the ingredients in a medium saucepan and bring to a boil. Simmer over low heat until deep golden brown and syrupy, about 15 minutes. • Drizzle the syrup over the baklava. • Serve warm or at room temperature.

10 sheets phyllo pastry,
   thawed if frozen
3 cups (300 g) chopped almonds
3 cups (300 g) chopped walnuts
1 tablespoon ground cinnamon
1 teaspoon ground cloves
$\frac{2}{3}$ cup (180 g) butter, melted

Syrup
$2\frac{1}{3}$ cups (450 g) sugar
$1\frac{1}{3}$ cups (310 ml) water
$\frac{1}{3}$ cup (90 g) honey
2 teaspoons lemon juice
$\frac{1}{2}$ teaspoon vanilla extract (essence)

Spirals
with golden raisins

Preheat the oven to 350°F (180°C/gas 4). • Grease 2 baking sheets. • Roll out the pastry on a lightly floured work surface to ¼ inch (5 mm) thick. • Spread with the pastry cream and sprinkle with the golden raisins. • Roll the pastry up into a log then cut into slices ½-inch (1-cm) thick. • Place the spirals on the prepared baking sheets and brush with some of the preserves. • Bake until golden brown, about 15 minutes. • Serve hot.

1 lb (500 g) frozen puff pastry, thawed
½ cup (125 g) golden raisins (sultanas)
1 quantity pastry cream (see page 34)
¼ cup (60 g) apricot preserves (jam), warmed

Apple Pastries

Preheat the oven to 350°F (180°C/gas 4). • Grease a large baking sheet. • Place the apples in a large bowl. Add the preserves, cinnamon, pine nuts, and golden raisins, and mix well. • Roll out the pastry on a lightly floured work surface to ¼ inch (5 mm) thick. • Cut the pastry into 4 inch (10 cm) squares. • Place a spoonful of the apple mixture in the center of each square and then fold them in half. Seal each one, pinching the edges of the pastry together. Make 3 incisions on the top of each pastry using a sharp knife. • Brush with the beaten egg yolk and arrange on the baking sheet. Sprinkle with the sugar granules. • Bake until well risen and golden brown, about 25 minutes. • Serve warm.

2 large apples, peeled, cored, and sliced
¼ cup (60 g) apricot preserves (jam)
1 teaspoon ground cinnamon
½ cup (100 g) pine kernels, coarsely chopped
½ cup (125 g) golden raisins (sultanas)
12 oz (350 g) frozen puff pastry, thawed
1 large egg yolk, lightly beaten
2 tablespoons sugar granules

47

Passion Fruit Tart

Preheat the oven to 350°F (180°C/gas 4). • Grease a 9-inch (23-cm) tart pan. • Pastry: Chop the flour, sugar, almonds, and butter in a food processor until the mixture resembles bread crumbs. Add the water and mix to make a smooth dough. • Roll out on a lightly floured work surface until $1/4$ inch (5 mm) thick. • Line the pan. Prick with a fork. Line with waxed paper and fill with dried beans. • Bake for 15 minutes. Remove the beans and bake until lightly browned, 15 minutes. Let cool. • Filling: Beat the egg yolks and sugar in a bowl until pale and creamy. • Add the passion fruit flesh. Transfer to a double boiler over barely simmering water and cook, stirring constantly, until thickened, 7–10 minutes. • Gradually add the butter. Remove from the heat and let cool. • Whip the cream in a large bowl until stiff. • Dissolve the gelatin in the water. Stir into the passion fruit mixture. Add the passion fruit mixture to the whipped cream. •

Spoon into the pastry case. Garnish with mandarin and passion fruit. • Chill for 1 hour before serving.

Pastry
1 cup (150 g) all-purpose (plain) flour
$1/4$ cup (50 g) g sugar
$1/3$ cup (30 g) finely ground almonds
$1/4$ cup (60 g) cold butter, cut up
3 tablespoons chilled water

Filling
6 large egg yolks
$1/4$ cup (50 g) sugar
3 oz (90 g) passion fruit flesh
$1/3$ cup (90 g) butter
$3/4$ cup (180 ml) heavy (double) cream
1 tablespoon gelatin powder
3 tablespoons boiling water
2 mandarins, peeled and sliced, to garnish
1 passion fruit, to garnish

SERVES 6–8

PREPARATION 20 min + 4 h to chill

DIFFICULTY level I

Yogurt Dessert
with mango and kiwi

Grease a 9 inch (23 cm) springform pan. • Put the sponge cake in the base of the pan and brush it with the rum. • Beat the yogurt and sugar in a large bowl until the sugar has dissolved. • Dissolve the gelatin in the boiling water in a cup. • Stir the gelatin into the yogurt mixture. • Pour the yogurt mixture over the sponge cake base. Cover and chill until the yogurt has set, about 3 hours. • Whip the cream in a large bowl until stiff. • Melt the preserves in a small saucepan over medium heat. • Remove the cake from the refrigerator and turn out on to a serving dish. • Spread with the cream. Make a ridged pattern around the sides using a fork. • Arrange the kiwi fruit and mango slices on top. Brush with the preserves. • Chill for 1 hour before serving.

- 1 (9-inch/23-cm) disk storebought sponge cake, about 1 inch (2.5 cm thick)
- 1/3 cup (90 ml) white rum
- 4 cups (1 kg) natural yogurt
- 1/2 cup (100 g) sugar
- 2 tablespoons gelatin powder
- 1/4 cup (60 ml) boiling water
- 1 cup (250 ml) heavy (double) cream
- 2 tablespoons apricot preserves (jam)
- 3 kiwi fruit, peeled and sliced
- 1 large ripe mango, pitted, and sliced

SERVES 6–8

PREPARATION 15 min + overnight to soak

COOKING 40 min

DIFFICULTY level 1

Apricot Cake
with pine nuts and cream

Put the apricots into a bowl and add the liqueur. Let soak overnight. Drain and chop finely. • Preheat the oven to 350°F (180°C/gas 4). • Grease a 10-inch (25-cm) cake pan. • Beat the sugar, honey, and butter in a large bowl until pale and creamy. • Add the eggs and egg yolks one at a time, beating until just combined after each addition. • Fold in the flour and baking powder and then the apricots. • Spoon the mixture into the prepared pan and sprinkle with the pine nuts. • Bake until lightly browned and springy to the touch, about 40 minutes. • Let cool slightly on a rack. • Serve warm with whipped cream.

8 oz (250 g) dried apricots
1/3 cup (90 ml) apricot liqueur
3/4 cup (150 g) sugar
1/3 cup (90 g) honey
1 cup (250 g) butter, softened
3 large eggs, lightly beaten
2 large egg yolks, lightly beaten
1 3/4 cups (275 g) all-purpose (plain) flour
1 teaspoon baking powder
1/2 cup (100 g) pine nuts
1 cup (250 ml) whipped cream, to serve

Coffee Roll

with walnuts

Preheat the oven to 400°F (200°C/gas 6). • Line a 10 x 15-inch (25 x 35-cm) jelly-roll pan with parchment paper. • Sponge: Sift the flour and cornstarch into a bowl. Add the walnuts and mix. • Beat the eggs and sugar in a large bowl until pale and creamy. • Fold in the mixed dry ingredients until well incorporated. • Spoon the mixture into the prepared pan. • Bake until golden brown and springy to the touch, 8–10 minutes. • Dust a clean kitchen towel with confectioners' sugar. Turn the cake out onto the towel and carefully remove the parchment paper. Roll up the cake, using the towel as a guide. Leave, seam side down, until cool. • Syrup: Heat the water and sugar in a small saucepan over medium heat. Cook until the sugar begins to caramelize, 5–7 minutes. Let cool slightly then stir in the rum. • Mocha cream: Mix the coffee, sugar, and rum in a small bowl, stirring until the sugar has dissolved. • Whip the cream in a small bowl until stiff. Fold in the coffee mixture. • Unroll the sponge and brush with the rum syrup. Spread with two-thirds of the mocha cream and then roll up again. • Transfer to a serving dish. Decorate with the remaining mocha cream and the walnuts. • Chill in the refrigerator for 1 hour before serving.

Sponge
1 cup (150 g) all-purpose (plain) flour
1 tablespoon cornstarch (cornflour)
1/4 cup (25 g) ground walnuts
3 large eggs
Generous 1/4 cup (60 g) sugar

Syrup
2 tablespoons water
2 teaspoons sugar
1 tablespoon rum

Mocha Cream
1 tablespoon instant coffee
2 tablespoons sugar
2 tablespoons rum
2/3 cup (150 ml) heavy (double) cream

To Decorate
18 walnuts

SERVES 6–8

PREPARATION 30 min + 2 h to chill

COOKING 15 min

DIFFICULTY level 3

Vanilla Roll

with chocolate cream

Preheat the oven to 350°F (180°C/gas 4). • Line a 10 x 15-inch (25 x 35-cm) jelly-roll pan with parchment paper. • Beat the egg yolks, confectioners' sugar, and vanilla in a large bowl until pale and creamy. • Fold in the flour and cornstarch. • Beat the egg whites and salt with an electric mixer at high speed until stiff. Gently fold them into the batter. • Spoon the batter into the prepared pan. • Bake for until risen and golden brown, about 15 minutes. • Dust a clean kitchen towel with confectioners' sugar. Turn the cake out onto the towel and carefully remove the parchment paper. Roll up the cake, using the towel as a guide. Leave, seam side down, until cool. • Unroll the sponge. Drizzle with the rum and cover with the chocolate spread. Roll up using the towel as a guide. Wrap the roll in foil. Chill for 2 hours. • Unwrap and transfer to a serving dish. • Dust with the confectioners' sugar and sprinkle with flakes of chocolate.

1 cup (150 g) confectioners' (icing) sugar + extra, to dust

4 large eggs, separated

⅓ cup (50 g) all-purpose (plain) flour

1 teaspoon vanilla extract (essence)

2 tablespoons cornstarch (cornflour)

⅛ teaspoon salt

3 tablespoons rum

½ cup (125 g) chocolate hazelnut spread (Nutella)

4 tablespoons dark chocolate flakes

SERVES 6–8

PREPARATION 45 min + 2 h to soak/chill

DIFFICULTY level 3

Raspberry Cream
layer cake

Place the raspberries, 1 cup (150 g) of confectioners' sugar, and kirsch in a large bowl. Soak for 1 hour. • Drain the raspberries, reserving the syrup. • Beat the cream cheese, remaining confectioners' sugar, and lemon zest in a large bowl until creamy. Mix in the raspberries. • Sprinkle the gelatin over the water in a saucepan. Let stand 1 minute. Stir over low heat until the gelatin has dissolved. • Beat the cream in a medium bowl until stiff. Fold the cream and the gelatin mixture into the raspberry mixture. • Split the cake in three horizontally. Place one layer on a serving plate. Brush with the syrup. Spread with half the raspberry mixture. Top with a second layer and spread with the remaining raspberry mixture. Top with the remaining layer. • Brush with the remaining syrup. • Heat the raspberry preserves in a saucepan until liquid. Spread over the cake. • Decorate with the raspberries. • Refrigerate for 1 hour before serving.

- 1 lb (500 g) raspberries (reserve 12 to decorate)
- 1⅔ cups (250 g) confectioners' (icing) sugar
- 1 cup (250 ml) kirsch
- 1 cup (250 g) cream cheese
- 1 tablespoon finely grated lemon zest
- 1¼ cups (310 ml) heavy (double) cream
- 2 tablespoons gelatin powder
- 4 tablespoons cold water
- 1 (9-inch/23-cm) sponge cake (homemade — see page 14 — or storebought)
- 1 cup (250 g) strained raspberry preserves (jam)

SERVES 6–8

PREPARATION 30 min

COOKING 45 min

DIFFICULTY level 2

Chocolate Cake

with cherry cream filling

Preheat the oven to 350°F (180°C/gas 4). • Butter two 9-inch (23-cm) round pans. • Sift the flour and baking powder into a large bowl. • Melt the chocolate and water in a double boiler over barely simmering water. • Beat the butter and brown sugar in a large bowl until creamy. • Add the eggs, one at a time, beating until just blended after each addition. • Gradually beat in the chocolate mixture, sour cream, and dry ingredients. • Spoon the batter into the prepared pans. • Bake until a toothpick inserted into the center comes out clean, 35–45 minutes. • Let cool in the pans on racks for 10 minutes. Turn out onto the racks and let cool completely. • Split the cakes horizontally. • Cherry Cream Filling: Mix the preserves and kirsch. • Beat the cream in a medium bowl until stiff. • Frosting: Stir together the confectioners' sugar and cocoa in a double boiler. Add the butter, vanilla, and enough of the water to make a firm paste. Stir over simmering water until smooth, about 3 minutes. • Place one layer of cake on a serving plate. Spread with one-third of the preserves and one-third of the whipped cream. Repeat with the remaining cake layers, finishing with a plain layer. • Spread the frosting over the top and sides of the cake. Decorate with the cherries.

1²⁄₃ cups (250 g) all-purpose (plain) flour
1¹⁄₂ teaspoons baking powder
5 oz (150 g) semisweet (dark) chocolate, chopped
¹⁄₂ cup (125 ml) water
¹⁄₂ cup (125 g) butter
1¹⁄₄ cups (250 g) firmly packed dark brown sugar
2 large eggs
¹⁄₂ cup (125 ml) sour cream

Cherry Cream Filling
1 cup (250 g) cherry preserves (jam)
3 tablespoons kirsch
2 cups (500 ml) heavy (double) cream

Chocolate Frosting
2 cups (300 g) confectioners' (icing) sugar
4 tablespoons unsweetened cocoa powder
2 tablespoons butter, softened
1 teaspoon vanilla extract (essence)
2–3 tablespoons boiling water

Candied cherries, to decorate

SERVES 8–10

PREPARATION 15 min + 1 h to rise

COOKING 30 min

DIFFICULTY level 2

Orange Fritters

Place the yeast a small bowl and stir in 4 tablespoons of the milk. Set aside for 15 minutes. • Sift the flour and salt into a large bowl. Stir in half the sugar, the Cointreau, and butter. Add the eggs one at a time and mix well. • Add the yeast mixture, orange zest, and remaining milk. Mix well. Cover and let rise in a warm place for 1 hour. • Heat the oil in a deep fryer or small, deep frying pan to very hot. • Drop spoonfuls of the batter into the oil and cook until golden brown all over, 3–5 minutes. Remove with a slotted spoon and drain on paper towels. • Sprinkle with the remaining sugar and serve hot.

1 oz (30 g) fresh yeast or 2 ($1/4$-oz/7-g) packages active dry yeast
1 cup (250 ml) milk, lukewarm
$3 1/3$ cups (500 g) all-purpose (plain) flour
Pinch of salt
$3/4$ cup (150 g) sugar
2 tablespoons Cointreau
$1/4$ cup (60 g) butter, melted
2 large eggs
Finely grated zest of 2 oranges
2 cups (500 ml) sunflower oil, for frying

60

Rice Fritters

with amaretti cookies

Place the milk in a large saucepan with the vanilla and salt. Add the flour and rice and mix well. • Bring to a boil over medium heat. Lower the heat and simmer, stirring often, until thick and the rice tender, 20–25 minutes. Remove from the heat. • Stir in the butter, half the sugar, 1 egg, and the amaretti cookies. • Turn the mixture out onto an oiled surface sprinkled with bread crumbs. Spread to ½ inch (1 cm) thick. Let cool. • Cut the mixture into disks using a 3-inch (8-cm) cookie cutter. • Beat the remaining egg in a small bowl. • Put the remaining bread crumbs on a plate. Dip the disks in the beaten egg and then in the bread crumbs, coating well. • Heat the oil in a large frying pan over medium heat. • Fry the fritters in small batches until golden brown all over, about 5 minutes per batch. Remove with a slotted spoon and drain on paper towels. • Sprinkle with the remaining sugar and serve hot.

2 cups (500 ml) milk
½ teaspoon vanilla extract (essence)
Pinch of salt
2 tablespoons all-purpose (plain) flour
½ cup (100 g) sticky rice
2 tablespoons butter
⅓ cup (70 g) sugar
2 large eggs
½ cup (60 g) crushed amaretti cookies (biscuits)
½ cup (60 g) fine dry bread crumbs
1 cup (250 ml) sunflower oil, for frying

SERVES 6–8

PREPARATION 15 min + 2 h to rest

COOKING 30 min

DIFFICULTY level 2

Pineapple Fritters

Place the pineapple in a bowl and drizzle with the lemon juice. Cover and set aside while you prepare the batter. • Sift the flour and the salt into a large bowl. Make well in the center and add the egg yolks, butter, and sugar. Mix well. • Gradually stir in the milk. Cover and let rest for 2 hours. • Beat the egg whites until stiff and fold into the batter. • Heat the oil in a deep fryer or small, deep frying pan to very hot. • Drain the pineapple slices well then dip them in the batter. • Fry in small batches until golden brown all over, 5–10 minutes per batch. • Remove with a slotted spoon and drain on paper towels. • Dust with confectioners' sugar and serve hot.

1 large ripe pineapple, peeled, sliced, and cored

Juice of 2 lemons

1²/₃ cups (250 g) all-purpose (plain) flour

Pinch of salt

2 large eggs, separated

2 tablespoons butter, melted

¹/₄ cup (50 g) sugar

Generous ³/₄ cup\200 ml milk

2 cups (500 ml) sunflower oil, for frying

4 tablespoons confectioners' (icing) sugar

Index

Copyright © 2007 by McRae Books Srl

This English edition first published in 2007

All rights reserved. No part of this book may be reproduced in any form without the prior written permission of the publisher and copyright owner.

Desserts

was created and produced by McRae Books Srl

Borgo Santa Croce, 8 – Florence (Italy)

info@mcraebooks.com

Publishers: Anne McRae and Marco Nardi

Project Director: Anne McRae

Design: Sara Mathews

Text: Carla Bardi

Editing: Osla Fraser

Photography: Mauro Corsi, Leonardo Pasquinelli, Gianni Petronio, Lorenzo Borri, Stefano Pratesi

Home Economist: Benedetto Rillo

Artbuying: McRae Books

Layouts: Adina Stefania Dragomir

Repro: Fotolito Raf, Florence

ISBN 978-88-89272-85-5

Printed and bound in China